Kurt Weill

Two Folksongs of the New Palestine

(1928)

For Voice and Piano

EA 851

EAM

EUROPEAN AMERICAN MUSIC
CORPORATION

FOREWORD

Jewish life and culture came under fierce attack in Europe in the 1930s. Anti-Semitism was on the rise, while the Jewish homeland espoused by Zionists remained a distant goal; no one knew that such a thing could be achieved. Nonetheless, an increasing number of Central European Jews were emigrating to Palestine, then a British protectorate, and forming their own communities there; in the process, they created a burgeoning musical culture. A musical literature consisting of new songs written by Jewish settlers had already sprung up. Keren Kayemeth (the Jewish National Fund) printed the texts and melodies of several of these songs on postcards and sent them to Jewish organizations around the world, in the hope of encouraging musical development and increasing emigration to Palestine. Using this raw material, German-Jewish musicologist Hans Nathan spearheaded the "Postcard Project" in the late 1930s, selecting existing songs for more elaborate compositional treatment.

Nathan's primary concern was creating a musical literature accessible to amateurs, but his standards were high. He asked well-known Jewish composers—many themselves refugees by this time—to create piano-vocal arrangements of the songs already being sung on kibbutzes (communal farms) in Palestine. He sent requests to a number of distinguished composers, including Aaron Copland, Paul Dessau, Arthur Honegger, Ernst Toch, Stefan Wolpe, and Kurt Weill, all of whom contributed settings. Nathan had collected thirty newly arranged songs by 1938, when they were published by Nigun Press in New York under the title "Folk Songs of the New Palestine."

Kurt Weill's parents and older brother had already left Nazi Germany to settle in Palestine. He responded quickly to Nathan, agreeing to arrange two of the songs, "Ba'a M'nucha" ("There Comes Peace") and "Havu l'venim" ("Bring the Bricks"). The songs are quite different. "Havu L'venim" is a vigorous work song, and Weill underpins its fast-moving melody with a characteristic, almost aggressive, march rhythm, as if urging the settlers to hasten to build a new society in Palestine. The accompaniment for the contemplative "Ba'a L'nucha" is much gentler, although Weill introduces tension into the left hand of the piano for the more disturbing third verse. However, he reverts to the previously established calm for the final refrain, and the overall effect of the song is one of peace and reassurance.

Dave Stein
Kurt Weill Foundation for Music
March 2008

I. Havu L'venim (Bring the Bricks)

הָבוּ לְבֵנִים,	Bring on the bricks
אֵין פְּנַאי לַעֲמֹד אַף רֶגַע!	There's no time to lose!
בְּנוּ הַבַּנָּאִים,	Builders – build,
אַל פַּחַד וְאַל יֶגַע!	Have no fear and never give up!
קִיר אֶל קִיר נָרִים	Wall by wall,
לִקְרַאת מִכְשׁוֹל וָפֶגַע.	we will build for tomorrow's setbacks and losses.

כֻּלָּנוּ נָשִׁיר	Together we shall sing
הִמְנוֹן בִּנְיַן אַרְצֵנוּ:	a song for building our land;
בִּמְקוֹם אֶתְמוֹל	Rather than yesterday,
יֵשׁ לָנוּ מָחָר	we have tomorrow;
וּבְעַד כָּל קִיר	the future of our people
בְּהֶנֶף בִּנְיָנֵנוּ	is our payment
עָתִיד עַמֵּנוּ	for each wall we build,
הוּא לָנוּ שָׂכָר.	with each wave of the arm.

הָבוּ, הָבוּ לְבֵנִים,	Bring, bring on the bricks
כְּפָר, מוֹשָׁב וָקֶרֶת!	every village, town and city!
שִׁירוּ זֶמֶר הַבּוֹנִים,	Sing the builders' song
שִׁיר בִּנְיָן וָמֶרֶד!	a song of building and rebellion!

II. Ba'a M'Nucha (There Comes Peace)

בָּאָה מְנוּחָה לַיָּגֵעַ	Peace comes to he who toils
וּמַרְגּוֹעַ לֶעָמֵל.	and rest to he who slaves away.
לַיְלָה חִוֵּר מִשְׂתָּרֵעַ	The pale night falls over
עַל שְׂדוֹת עֵמֶק יִזְרְעֶאל.	the fields of the Jezreel Valley.
טַל מִלְּמַטָּה וּלְבָנָה מֵעַל	Dew from below and the moon above
מִבֵּית-אַלְפָא עַד נַהֲלָל.	from Beit Alfa to Nahalal.

(ed. note: Beit Alfa and Nahalal are names of Kibbutzim in the Jezreel Valley)

מַה, מַה, לַיְלָה מִלֵּיל?	What is there, night after night?
דְּמָמָה בְּיִזְרְעֶאל.	Silence in the Valley.
נוּמָה, עֵמֶק, אֶרֶץ, תִּפְאֶרֶת,	Rest, valley, glorious land,
אָנוּ לָךְ מִשְׁמֶרֶת.	We are here to watch over you.

יָם הַדָּגָן מִתְנוֹעֵעַ	The grain sways;
שִׁיר הָעֵדֶר מְצַלְצֵל.	the song of the flock fills the air.
זוֹהִי אַרְצִי וּשְׂדוֹתֶיהָ,	This is my land and its fields,
זֶהוּ עֵמֶק יִזְרְעֶאל.	this is the Jezreel Valley.
תְּבוֹרַךְ אַרְצִי וְתִתְהַלָּל	Bless you, my land; may you be praised,
מִבֵּית-אַלְפָא עַד נַהֲלָל.	from Beit Alfa to Nahalal.

מַה, מַה, לַיְלָה מִלֵּיל...	What is there, night after night? *(refrain...)*

אֹפֶל בְּהַר הַגִּלְבֹּעַ,	Mount Gilboa is dark now;
סוּס דּוֹהֵר מִצֵּל אֶל צֵל.	horses gallop from one shadow to the next.
קוֹל זְעָקָה עָף גָּבוֹהַּ,	A sound rings out to the heavens,
מִשְּׂדוֹת עֵמֶק יִזְרְעֶאל.	from the fields of the Valley of Jezreel.
מִי יָרָה וּמִי זֶה שָׁם נָפַל,	Who pulled the trigger, and who fell dead,
בֵּין בֵּית-אַלְפָא וְנַהֲלָל?	between Beit Alfa and Nahalal?

מַה, מַה, לַיְלָה מִלֵּיל...	What is there, night after night? *(refrain...)*

Translation by:
Aviah Morag

Havu L'venim

(Bring the Bricks)

Melody: Mordechai Zaira
Words: Alexander Penn

ARR. KURT WEILL

Alla marcia, un poco tenuto

Ha-vu l' ve-nim,   en

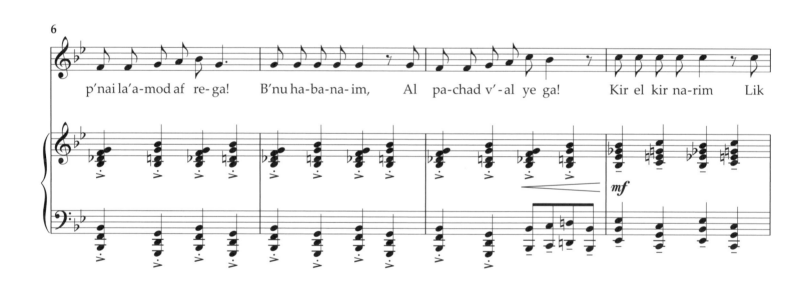

p'nai la'a-mod af re-ga! B'nu ha-ba-na-im,   Al   pa-chad v'-al ye ga!   Kir el kir na-rim   Lik

rat mich shol va-fe-ga. Kul - la - nu na-shir,   Him nom bin-yan ar tze-nu: Bin kom   et - mol   Yesh

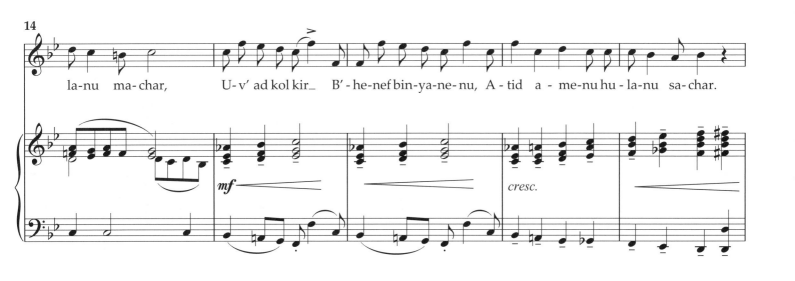

la- nu ma- char, U- v' ad kol kir_ B'- he-nef bin-ya-ne-nu, A - tid a - me-nu hu - la-nu sa-char.

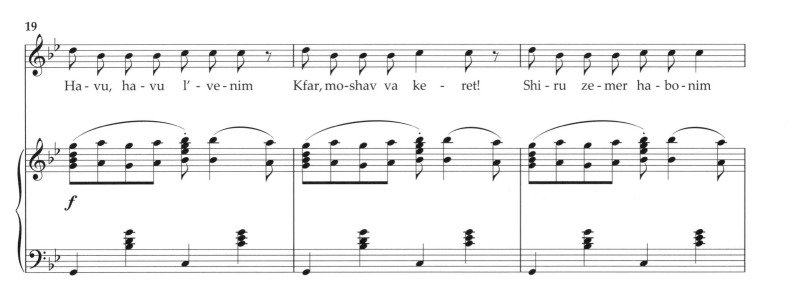

Ha - vu, ha - vu l'- ve- nim Kfar, mo-shav va ke - ret! Shi - ru ze - mer ha - bo - nim

1. Shir bin - yan va - me - red! **2.** *rit.* Shir bin - yan va - me - red!

BA'-A M'NUCHA

(There Comes Peace)

Melody: Daniel Sanbursky
Words: Nathan Alterman

Shir Haemek
(Song of the Valley)
ARR. KURT WEILL

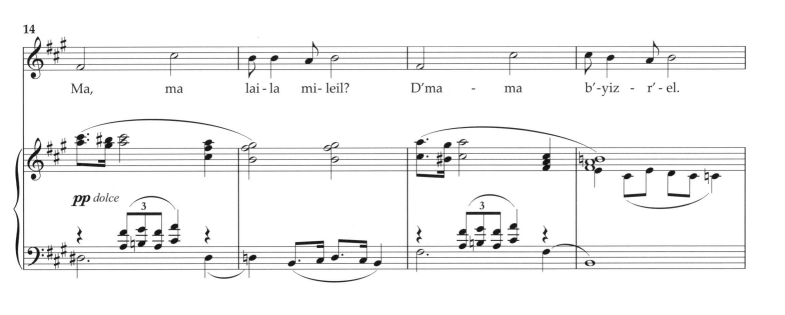

14

Ma, ma lai - la mi - leil? D'ma - ma b'yiz - r' - el.

pp dolce

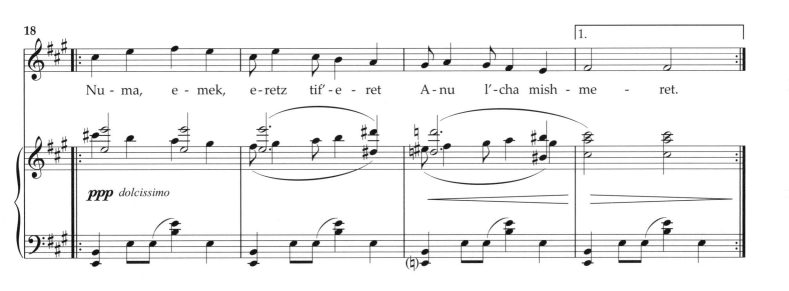

18

Nu - ma, e - mek, e - retz tif' - e - ret A - nu l'cha mish - me - ret.

ppp dolcissimo

1.

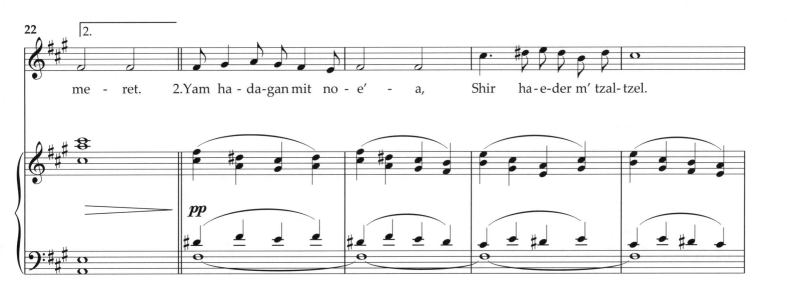

22

2.

me - ret. 2. Yam ha - da - gan mit no - e' - a, Shir ha - e - der m' tzal - tzel.

pp

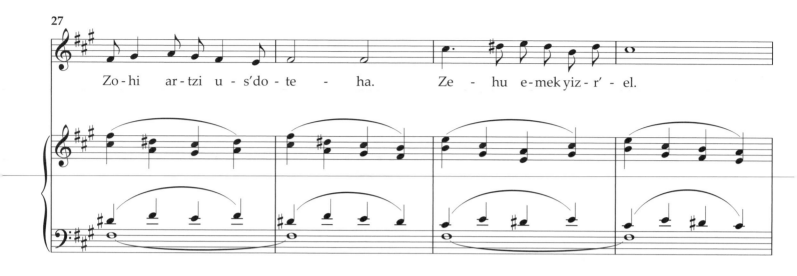

Zo - hi ar - tzi u - s'do - te - ha. Ze - hu e - mek yiz - r' - el.

T' - vo - rach ar - tzi v - tit - ha - lal, Mi - beit - al - fa ad na - ha - lal.

Ma, ma lai - la mi - leil? D'ma - ma b - yiz - r' - el.

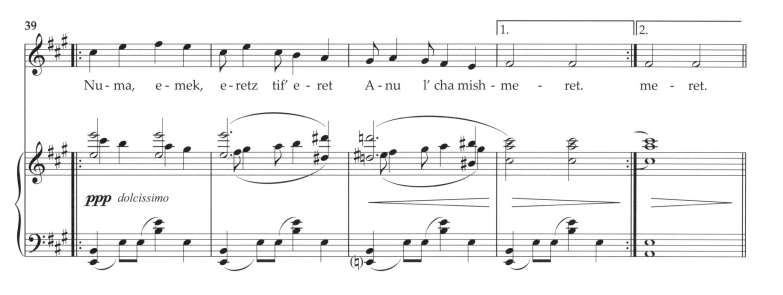

Nu - ma, e - mek, e - retz tif' e - ret A - nu l' cha mish - me - ret. me - ret.

ppp dolcissimo

3. O - fel b' har ha gil - bo - a, Sus do-her mi-tzel el tzel.

mf

Kol z' - a-ka af ga-vo - a, Mi - s'dot e-mek yiz-r' - el.

mf

Mi - ya - ra u - mi zeh sham na - fal Bein beit - al - fa

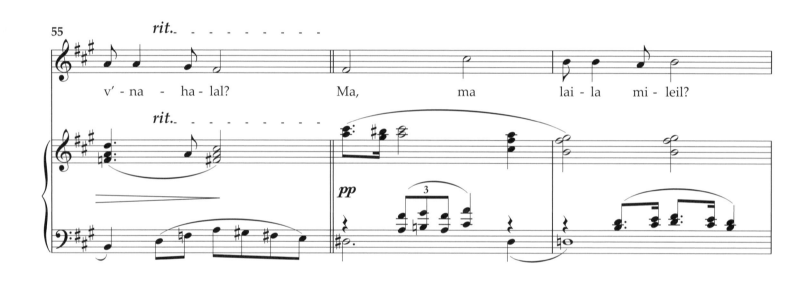

v' - na - ha - lal? Ma, ma lai - la mi - leil?

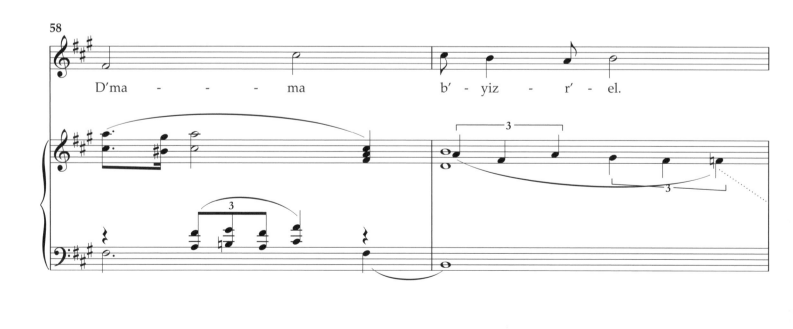

D'ma - - ma b' - yiz - r' - el.